I0005129

MASTERING LLM
ENGINEERING

A Practical Guide to Building
and Optimizing Local AI
Models for Smart Apps

TABLE OF CONTENTS

- The role of NLP in LLMs

- How LLMs generate human-like responses

● **Chapter 3: Setting Up the LLM Engineering Environment**

3.1 Choosing the Right Tools and Frameworks

- Overview of key LLM engineering frameworks (TensorFlow, PyTorch, etc.)

- Tools for local deployment of LLMs

3.2 Setting Up Your Development Environment

- Step-by-step guide to setting up LLM development tools

- Best practices for managing dependencies

3.3 First Steps with LLM Models

- Running your first LLM in a local environment

- Simple examples to get started

● **Chapter 4: Building Your First Local LLM**

4.1 Selecting a Pre-trained Model

- How to choose the right pre-trained model for your app

- Pros and cons of different pre-trained models

4.2 Setting Up Local Deployment

- How to deploy your first model locally

- Integrating your local LLM with an app

4.3 Testing and Evaluating the Model

- Performance benchmarks

- Understanding model outputs and tuning the results

● **Chapter 5: Customizing and Optimizing Local LLMs**

5.1 Fine-Tuning LLMs for Specific Tasks

- Techniques for adapting models to your app's needs

- Training with domain-specific data

5.2 Optimizing Model Size for Local Deployment

- Reducing model size without compromising accuracy

- Using model compression techniques (pruning, quantization)

- How local deployment reduces the risk of data breaches

7.2 Security Measures for Local LLM Apps

- Encryption and secure data handling techniques

- Managing and protecting sensitive data in local models

7.3 Compliance with Data Regulations

- GDPR, CCPA, and other privacy standards

- How to design LLM-powered apps that comply with regulations

- **Chapter 8: Troubleshooting and Debugging LLM Apps**

8.1 Common Issues in LLM Engineering

- Memory errors, performance bottlenecks, and other challenges

- Debugging strategies for local LLM-powered apps

8.2 Handling Model Inaccuracies

- Identifying and correcting flawed model outputs

- Fine-tuning to improve accuracy and relevance

8.3 Testing for Robustness

- Techniques for stress testing and ensuring app stability

- How to handle edge cases and unexpected inputs

- **Chapter 9: Scaling Local LLM Solutions**

9.1 Strategies for Scaling Local Models

- When and how to scale your local LLM app

- Managing resource usage as your app grows

9.2 Handling Increased User Demand

- Strategies for optimizing performance under high load

- Distributed computing for scaling LLM-powered apps

9.3 Optimizing for Cross-Platform Deployment

- Ensuring compatibility across mobile, web, and desktop environments

- Deploying apps with local LLMs across multiple devices

- **Chapter 10: The Future of LLM Engineering and Smart Applications**

10.1 Emerging Trends in LLM Engineering

- What's next in LLM development?

- Advances in model architectures and optimization techniques

10.2 Opportunities in Various Industries

- How local LLMs are revolutionizing industries like healthcare, finance, and customer service

10.3 Building a Career in LLM Engineering

- Skills and resources for aspiring LLM engineers

- Career opportunities in LLM-based app development

● Conclusion

- Recap of Key Insights

- Final thoughts on LLM engineering and its impact on the future of app development

- Encouragement to Start Developing with LLMs

- Call to action for readers to begin their own LLM projects and dive deeper into the world of local AI applications

INTRODUCTION

Large Language Models (LLMs) are one of the most significant advancements in artificial intelligence (AI) in recent years. These models, built on deep learning frameworks, have the ability to process and generate human-like text. As the demand for smarter applications increases, developers are turning to LLMs to create more intuitive, conversational, and responsive systems. LLM engineering, therefore, becomes a crucial area of expertise for anyone looking to integrate AI into their applications effectively.

In this guide, we will explore the core concepts of LLM engineering, understand the structure and workings of these models, and examine why local LLMs are an essential aspect of future app development. Additionally, this book will provide readers with the skills required to deploy, optimize, and scale LLM-based applications.

● **Overview of LLM Engineering**

LLM engineering refers to the practice of designing, deploying, and optimizing large language models. These models are based on neural networks and utilize a variety of architectures to understand and generate human language. The most well-known models, such as GPT-3, BERT, and T5, have demonstrated an ability to perform tasks like translation, summarization, and even question answering with remarkable accuracy. At the core of LLM engineering is a deep understanding of how these models process language. This involves a significant amount of data training, fine-tuning, and optimization to make these models not just functional, but efficient and scalable for real-world use. In the past few years, LLMs have become more powerful, and with the increased computing power available today, they can be deployed locally on devices, offering a new paradigm in AI application development.

The advent of local LLMs marks a shift away from cloud-based models. This transition allows developers to deploy AI systems that are more autonomous, faster, and secure. By using local LLMs, developers can create applications that perform tasks like conversational AI, real-time data processing, and user personalization directly on users' devices.

- **Understanding Large Language Models (LLMs)**

Large Language Models are built on transformer architectures that excel at processing sequences of data, such as text. These models are trained on vast amounts of text data, which allows them to capture the nuances of language, including grammar, context, and meaning. The transformer architecture, introduced by Vaswani et al. in 2017, relies heavily on a mechanism called self-attention. This allows the model to weigh the importance of each word in a sentence relative to others, enabling it to generate more coherent and contextually relevant outputs. Training a large language model requires massive datasets and significant computational resources. These models learn by predicting the next word in a sequence, given the preceding words. As they process more text, they become better at understanding language patterns. Fine-tuning is the next step, where a pre-trained model is adapted to a specific domain, task, or application. For example, a model trained on general internet data can be fine-tuned to perform tasks related to legal or medical texts.

The scale of these models is what gives them their power. LLMs like GPT-3 contain billions of parameters, which allows them to generate high-quality text outputs. The large parameter count enables the model to represent a more detailed understanding of language, making it versatile across a range of tasks, from simple text generation to complex problem-solving. LLMs are typically built with layers of attention heads and feed-forward networks that process information in parallel, which makes them particularly effective for tasks that require both long-range dependencies and real-time processing. The large scale of these models, however, also introduces challenges related to computational efficiency, model size, and deployment.

- **Why Local LLMs are the Future of App Development**

Traditionally, large language models were deployed on cloud-based servers, where the computation-intensive processes could be managed with high-powered hardware. However, this approach comes with significant drawbacks, such as latency, data privacy concerns, and dependency on internet connectivity. Local LLMs, which can be deployed directly on end-user devices, offer several key advantages that make them an appealing choice for app developers.

- Reduced Latency: Local LLMs allow for real-time processing and responses without needing to rely on a remote server. This reduces the latency typically associated with cloud-based systems, where data must travel between the device and the server, often introducing a noticeable delay. By running models locally, developers can create faster, more responsive applications. Improved Data Privacy: Privacy concerns are one of the major issues when using cloud-based AI systems. When user data is sent to a remote server, it can potentially be exposed to security vulnerabilities or unauthorized access. Local LLMs mitigate these risks by processing data on the device itself, ensuring that sensitive information is never transmitted externally.

- Offline Functionality: Many applications, especially those in remote or underserved areas, need to function without a reliable internet connection. Local LLMs allow for offline functionality, ensuring that users can continue interacting with AI-powered applications even in situations where connectivity is limited or nonexistent.

- Customization and Control: Local LLMs provide developers with greater flexibility to fine-tune models to meet the specific needs of an application. With cloud-based models, developers are often limited to the functionality and customization options provided by the service. On the other hand, local deployment allows for full control over the model's architecture, training process, and performance tuning.

In addition, local models can be more easily optimized for specific hardware configurations, ensuring that they run efficiently on mobile phones, laptops, or edge devices. This leads to better resource management, reduced power consumption, and improved battery life, which is critical for applications running on mobile devices.

● **Purpose and Scope of the Book**

This book aims to provide a comprehensive guide to LLM engineering, focusing on the practical aspects of developing, deploying, and optimizing local language models for real-world applications. It is designed for developers, AI enthusiasts, and app creators who want to understand how to integrate LLMs into their applications effectively, without relying on cloud-based solutions. The primary purpose of this book is to equip readers with the knowledge and skills required to build, deploy, and scale LLM-powered applications. Throughout the chapters, we will explore the theoretical foundations of LLMs, followed by practical steps to implement and optimize these models for local environments. Readers will gain insights into the challenges of local deployment, as well as strategies for overcoming these obstacles.

- **By the end of this book, readers will be able to:**

1. Understand the key concepts and technologies behind LLMs.

2. Set up a local development environment for LLM deployment.

3. Build and fine-tune models for specific tasks and applications.

4. Optimize LLMs for performance and efficiency.

5. Integrate LLMs into smart applications, focusing on usability, security, and scalability.

6. Troubleshoot and debug LLM-based systems.

7. Scale local LLM apps to handle increased demand.

This guide is not only intended to be a technical manual, but also a roadmap for developers looking to stay at the forefront of AI application development.

- **Who This Book is For**

This book is specifically designed for software developers and AI enthusiasts who are interested in learning how to integrate large language models into their applications. Whether you're building conversational agents, smart assistants, or applications that require sophisticated language processing capabilities, this book will provide you with the tools and knowledge to implement these models effectively. It is also suitable for those who are already familiar with AI but want to delve deeper into the specifics of local LLM deployment. Understanding the challenges and solutions involved in localizing these models is critical for developers seeking to optimize performance and improve user experience.

Additionally, app creators who wish to leverage LLM technology for enhancing user interfaces, enabling natural language interactions, and improving overall app intelligence will find this book invaluable.

● What You Will Learn and Accomplish

By following the chapters of this book, readers will gain a clear understanding of LLM engineering, from the theoretical background to the practical application. You will explore the architecture and design of large language models and learn how to deploy them locally for a range of real-world use cases.

● Key outcomes of this book include:

1. Proficiency in setting up an LLM engineering environment.

2. Knowledge of pre-trained models and how to select the best one for your app.

3. Skills to fine-tune LLMs for specific tasks and applications.

4. Strategies for optimizing local LLM performance.

5. Best practices for integrating LLMs into mobile, web, and desktop applications.

6. Expertise in securing data and ensuring privacy with local models.

7. Techniques for troubleshooting and debugging LLM applications.

8. Understanding how to scale and optimize local solutions for different platforms and user demands.

● **How This Book is Structured**

This book is structured to take readers through a step-by-step process of mastering LLM engineering, from understanding the core principles to deploying and optimizing models for real-world use. Each chapter is designed to build upon the last, gradually advancing the reader's understanding and practical abilities.

The structure includes:

1. Foundational Concepts: Understanding the underlying technologies and theories that power large language models.

2. Hands-on Projects: Practical examples and case studies demonstrating the application of LLMs in real-world scenarios.

3. Optimization and Scaling: Techniques for making LLMs work efficiently in local environments, ensuring they can handle increasing user demands and resource constraints.

4. Integration into Applications: A focus on integrating LLMs into modern apps with a focus on usability, security, and scalability.

The book also includes additional resources, such as code snippets, exercises, and reference materials, designed to enhance the learning experience and provide ongoing support as you work through the projects.

Chapter 1

Introduction to LLM Engineering

1.1 What are Large Language Models?

Large Language Models (LLMs) are a type of artificial intelligence designed to process and generate human language. These models are trained on vast datasets containing billions of words and are designed to understand, generate, and manipulate text with a level of complexity that simulates human-like language comprehension and production. At their core, LLMs leverage neural networks, specifically deep learning techniques, to model relationships between words, phrases, and entire sentences. This allows them to grasp not only the meaning of individual words but also the intricate structures and contextual nuances that come with human language.

The underlying architecture of an LLM typically includes millions or even billions of parameters. These parameters are the result of training the model on massive datasets, such as books, websites, and other text corpora. The training process involves adjusting the weights of connections within the model's neural network in a way that enables it to predict the likelihood of a word or phrase following another. This training allows LLMs to handle a variety of tasks, such as translation, text generation, summarization, and question answering.

One of the defining features of LLMs is the use of transformers—an architecture that employs attention mechanisms. This allows the model to weigh the importance of different parts of the input text, regardless of their position. Traditional machine learning models, on the other hand, tend to focus on sequential processing (e.g., one word at a time in a sentence) and may struggle with long-range dependencies within the text. Transformers enable LLMs to capture the broader context of a sentence or passage, making them highly effective for understanding and generating natural language. Compared to traditional machine learning models, LLMs represent a shift in how machines process information. While older models relied on predefined rules and shallow patterns to process text, LLMs learn from massive amounts of unstructured data and adapt to new tasks without explicit programming. This results in significantly more flexible and robust models capable of understanding and generating text across various domains without the need for task-specific adjustments.

1.2 The Evolution of LLMs

The development of LLMs has been a progressive journey of improvement in natural language processing (NLP). Early NLP models focused on rule-based systems and relied on explicitly defined structures to understand language. These systems had limited scope and struggled with ambiguity and context, which are inherent in natural language. As computational power grew, statistical models emerged that could infer patterns from large datasets, leading to a more flexible approach to language understanding. The breakthrough in LLMs occurred with the introduction of deep learning. Deep neural networks, particularly recurrent neural networks (RNNs) and long short-term memory (LSTM) networks, enabled the modeling of sequential data, such as sentences or paragraphs. However, these models had limitations when dealing with long-range dependencies in text. The true game-changer came with the introduction of the transformer architecture in 2017. Proposed by Vaswani et al. in the paper "Attention is All You Need," the transformer revolutionized NLP by replacing traditional sequence processing mechanisms with a self-attention mechanism. This architecture allowed models to process words in parallel, improving efficiency and enabling better performance on tasks such as translation and text generation. The self-attention mechanism in transformers enabled models to consider the importance of each word in relation to every other word in the input, thus overcoming the limitations of earlier models. Following the introduction of the transformer, several key LLMs emerged that set new benchmarks for performance. BERT (Bidirectional Encoder Representations from Transformers), introduced by Google in 2018, brought a new paradigm to language modeling by pre-training on vast corpora and then fine-tuning for specific tasks. Unlike previous models that processed text in a left-to-right or right-to-left manner, BERT used a bidirectional approach, which significantly improved its ability to understand context and meaning. BERT's success led to the rise of a variety of transformer-based models designed for a wide range of applications.

Another milestone in LLM development was the release of GPT (Generative Pretrained Transformer) models by OpenAI. The first version, GPT, was trained using a unidirectional transformer model for autoregressive text generation, meaning it predicted the next word in a sentence based on the preceding words. Over time, OpenAI released increasingly larger versions, culminating in GPT-3, which boasts 175 billion parameters. GPT-3 is capable of generating highly coherent and contextually relevant text across a wide range of tasks, from writing essays to generating code.

The success of GPT-3 and similar models, such as T5 (Text-to-Text Transfer Transformer) and XLNet, further solidified the position of transformers as the dominant architecture in NLP. These models demonstrated remarkable capabilities in understanding and generating text, setting new standards for benchmarks across various NLP tasks.

However, the rapid growth in model size also raised concerns about efficiency, ethical implications, and accessibility. Models like GPT-3 require immense computational resources for both training and inference, leading to increased interest in finding more efficient ways to deploy these models while maintaining their performance.

1.3 Why Local LLMs?

With the growing sophistication of LLMs, a key question has emerged: should these models be deployed locally on user devices or run in the cloud? Cloud-based LLMs have become a standard for many applications due to their ability to provide on-demand, powerful AI without the need for extensive local hardware. However, there are several compelling reasons why deploying LLMs locally can be a more attractive solution in certain scenarios. One of the most significant advantages of local LLMs is data privacy and security. With cloud-based models, sensitive data often needs to be sent to remote servers for processing. This raises concerns about data leakage, breaches, and the possibility of surveillance. Local deployment ensures that data can be processed directly on the device, without ever leaving it. This is particularly important for industries that deal with sensitive or personal data, such as healthcare, finance, and legal sectors, where privacy is a top priority. By keeping data local, organizations can comply with strict regulations such as GDPR and HIPAA while ensuring the security of their users.

Another major benefit of local LLMs is latency reduction. Cloud-based models typically require internet access, and the round-trip time for data to travel from the user's device to the server and back can introduce significant delays. This can be a bottleneck for real-time applications, such as conversational agents, virtual assistants, or autonomous systems. By processing data locally, these delays are minimized, resulting in faster response times and smoother user experiences. Cost efficiency is another reason why local LLMs are becoming increasingly appealing. Cloud providers often charge based on the amount of computational resources consumed, which can become expensive, especially for applications with high usage. Local deployment eliminates ongoing cloud service fees, offering more predictable and often lower costs for organizations in the long run. In addition to these practical benefits, local LLMs provide a level of control that cloud-based models cannot match. When running models locally, developers have the ability to fine-tune and optimize the models for specific use cases and environments. This flexibility is particularly important for applications that require high levels of customization, such as specialized chatbots, personal assistants, or industry-specific tools. Local deployment also allows for greater control over the model's behavior, such as limiting its scope or ensuring it adheres to certain ethical guidelines.

Local LLMs also benefit from the increasing advancements in hardware. Modern smartphones, edge devices, and personal computers are becoming more powerful, with specialized hardware such as Graphics Processing Units (GPUs) and Tensor Processing Units (TPUs) enabling local AI processing at a scale previously reserved for the cloud. With advancements in model compression and optimization techniques, it is now feasible to run even large-scale models on local devices without sacrificing too much performance. The use cases for local LLM-powered applications are vast. For instance, voice assistants like Apple's Siri or Google Assistant are increasingly using local processing to handle voice commands in real-time without needing to send data to the cloud. Similarly, mobile applications for translation, document summarization, and content generation can benefit from local LLM deployment, ensuring faster performance and a better user experience. In industries like automotive, where autonomous driving systems need to process vast amounts of sensor data and provide real-time feedback, local LLMs are poised to play a critical role in enhancing safety and performance. While local deployment has its advantages, it is not without challenges. Local LLMs require significant resources in terms of memory, processing power, and storage, which may not be available on all devices. Moreover, optimizing models to run efficiently on resource-constrained devices remains a key area of research and development. Nonetheless, the combination of hardware advancements and software optimizations is making local LLMs a viable option for a growing number of applications, presenting exciting opportunities for developers and companies alike. In summary, Large Language Models have evolved from simple statistical methods to powerful deep learning systems capable of sophisticated language understanding and generation. The advent of transformers has significantly improved the performance of these models, and with increasing interest in local deployment, LLMs are poised to reshape the future of AI-powered applications. Local LLMs, with their advantages in privacy, latency, cost, and control, offer a promising alternative to cloud-based models, and their use cases are rapidly expanding across industries. As LLMs continue to improve, the possibilities for local deployment are becoming even more compelling, setting the stage for a new era of smart, AI-powered applications.

Chapter 2

Understanding the Core Components of LLMs

2.1 The Anatomy of an LLM

Large Language Models (LLMs) are based on neural networks, specifically deep learning architectures, which have revolutionized the field of artificial intelligence. Neural networks are composed of interconnected layers of artificial neurons that process information in a hierarchical fashion, mimicking the structure of biological neural networks in the human brain. LLMs utilize deep neural networks, which are networks with many layers between the input and output. The deeper the network, the more abstract and complex the representations of the data become. The most prominent neural network architecture in the context of LLMs is the Transformer. The

Transformer model, introduced by Vaswani et al. in 2017, fundamentally changed the way natural language processing (NLP) tasks are approached. Unlike previous models that processed data sequentially (such as Recurrent Neural Networks or RNNs), Transformers operate by processing all input data simultaneously through a mechanism known as attention.

- **Understanding Transformers and Attention Mechanisms**

Transformers are based on self-attention mechanisms that allow the model to weigh the relevance of different words in a sentence, regardless of their position. This is achieved through the attention mechanism, which calculates a set of weights that indicate the importance of each word in a given context. For example, in the sentence "The cat sat on the mat," the model can learn to pay more attention to the relationship between "cat" and "sat" than between "the" and "mat."

The Transformer consists of two main components: the encoder and the decoder. In LLMs like GPT (Generative Pre-trained Transformer), only the decoder part of the Transformer is used. The encoder-decoder architecture is commonly used for tasks like machine translation, while the decoder-only architecture is more suited for text generation, as seen in models like GPT-3 and GPT-4. Each of these components is composed of multiple layers, where each layer performs self-attention and other transformations to refine the representation of the input data. This approach allows LLMs to process long-range dependencies in language more effectively than previous architectures, enabling them to generate coherent and contextually accurate text over long passages. The self-attention mechanism also supports parallel processing, making Transformers significantly faster to train compared to earlier models.

2.2 Pre-training and Fine-tuning

LLMs, particularly those like GPT, undergo two primary phases of training: pre-training and fine-tuning. These phases allow the model to learn from vast amounts of data before adapting to more specific tasks.

● **How LLMs Are Trained**

Pre-training is the first phase where an LLM learns general language patterns. This is done by feeding the model massive datasets composed of text from diverse sources, such as books, websites, and articles. The objective during pre-training is for the model to predict the next word in a sequence of text. This task is known as language modeling, and the model is trained by comparing its predictions to the actual next words in the training data. Pre-training allows the model to acquire a broad understanding of language, grammar, facts, and even some degree of reasoning. The more data and computational power used during pre-training, the more sophisticated the model becomes in understanding the structure and intricacies of language. The model learns to capture relationships between words, sentences, and paragraphs, gaining an ability to predict and generate realistic and coherent text.

- **Techniques for Adapting Models to Specific Tasks**

Once pre-training is complete, fine-tuning is employed to adapt the model to specific tasks or domains. In fine-tuning, the pre-trained model is further trained on a smaller, task-specific dataset. For example, if the goal is to create a chatbot, the model might be fine-tuned on a conversational dataset to improve its ability to respond in a human-like manner. The fine-tuning process often involves supervised learning, where the model is provided with labeled data to learn how to map input text to desired outputs.

Fine-tuning is crucial for improving the model's performance on specialized tasks like sentiment analysis, question answering, or summarization. By adjusting the model's weights based on task-specific data, the model can make more accurate predictions and generate more relevant outputs. Fine-tuning is typically less computationally expensive than pre-training since it involves working with a smaller dataset, but it is equally essential for optimizing performance in specific applications.

2.3 Language Understanding and Generation

LLMs excel in both understanding and generating natural language, which makes them versatile tools in NLP. Their capability to engage in coherent dialogue, summarize information, and answer questions relies on their deep understanding of language structure, meaning, and context.

- **The Role of NLP in LLMs**

Natural Language Processing (NLP) is a subfield of AI focused on enabling machines to understand and generate human language. LLMs are built on NLP principles, allowing them to process and analyze vast amounts of text in a way that is contextually aware and semantically accurate. At a fundamental level, NLP tasks involve breaking down language into components such as words, phrases, and sentences, then interpreting their relationships and meanings. LLMs leverage the vast amounts of text they were trained on to discern syntactic patterns, semantic nuances, and contextual dependencies. These models can, for example, identify the subject of a sentence, resolve ambiguous pronouns, and interpret figurative language. The ability to understand context is particularly important in natural language generation tasks, where the model must generate coherent and relevant responses based on prior input.

- **How LLMs Generate Human-Like Responses**

The generation of human-like responses by LLMs relies on their ability to predict the next word or phrase in a sequence, based on prior context. During inference (the process of using a trained model to make predictions), LLMs use the patterns learned during training to generate text. The model begins with a prompt or an initial sequence of words and then predicts the most probable next word, repeating this process until it generates a full sentence, paragraph, or response. The generative capabilities of LLMs are enhanced by the attention mechanism discussed earlier. As the model generates each word, it recalculates attention weights to focus on the most relevant parts of the input context. This ensures that the generated text remains coherent and contextually appropriate.

LLMs are also capable of performing "zero-shot" and "few-shot" learning. In zero-shot learning, the model can generate relevant responses or perform tasks without being explicitly trained on that specific task. In few-shot learning, the model is given a few examples of a task and can then generalize from those examples to handle similar tasks. This adaptability allows LLMs to handle a wide range of use cases without the need for task-specific training data.

The ability to generate fluent, contextually accurate text has made LLMs invaluable in applications like chatbots, content generation, and automated summarization. Their capacity to maintain context over extended conversations or documents, combined with their understanding of grammar, meaning, and tone, allows them to generate responses that are not only syntactically correct but also semantically meaningful.

Chapter 3

Setting Up the LLM Engineering Environment

3.1 Choosing the Right Tools and Frameworks

When it comes to large language models (LLMs), selecting the right tools and frameworks is crucial for building efficient and scalable systems. A variety of options exist, but two of the most widely used frameworks for training and deploying LLMs are TensorFlow and PyTorch. These frameworks provide robust environments for building machine learning models, especially those involving deep learning architectures like transformers that power LLMs.

- TensorFlow

Developed by Google, TensorFlow is a powerful and flexible machine learning framework. It provides an extensive set of libraries and tools for model development, training, and deployment. TensorFlow's key strength lies in its scalability, making it ideal for both research and production environments. It supports distributed computing, and with TensorFlow Lite, it can be optimized for running models on mobile devices. TensorFlow's high-level API, Keras, allows for easy model building with simple and understandable code, making it suitable for developers with varying levels of expertise.

- PyTorch

PyTorch, developed by Facebook, is another highly popular framework for building deep learning models. PyTorch's main advantage lies in its dynamic computational graph, which is more intuitive and flexible compared to TensorFlow's static graph (prior to TensorFlow 2.0). This dynamic nature allows developers to modify the model architecture during runtime, which is especially useful for research and experimentation. PyTorch also boasts a seamless integration with Python, making it a favorite among developers who prioritize flexibility and ease of use. Additionally, it is highly compatible with CUDA, making it suitable for high-performance GPU computations.

Other Tools and Frameworks

While TensorFlow and PyTorch dominate the landscape, other tools may also play a role depending on the deployment environment. For local deployment of LLMs, it's essential to consider libraries and tools designed for optimization. These include:

- Hugging Face Transformers: A popular library for working with transformer models, it simplifies the process of fine-tuning pre-trained models like GPT-2, BERT, and others. Hugging Face's ecosystem has become indispensable for most developers working with LLMs due to its rich community support and pre-trained models.

- ONNX (Open Neural Network Exchange): ONNX is an open-source format designed to enable models to be transferred between different machine learning frameworks, such as TensorFlow and PyTorch. This format helps simplify deployment processes and ensures compatibility across environments.

- TensorFlow Lite and PyTorch Mobile: For local deployment on mobile devices, these frameworks provide optimized versions of

TensorFlow and PyTorch, which reduce memory and computational demands while maintaining performance.

3.2 Setting Up Your Development Environment

Once the framework has been chosen, setting up the development environment is the next step. Below is a step-by-step guide to setting up a local LLM development environment using both PyTorch and TensorFlow.

Step 1: Install the Necessary Dependencies

Before you can begin developing with LLMs, you need to set up the development environment and install the necessary dependencies. Start by setting up a Python environment to manage libraries and dependencies.

1. Install Python (preferably Python 3.7 or above).

2. Set up a virtual environment to avoid conflicts with other Python projects. This can be done with the following command:

python -m venv llm_env

3. Activate the virtual environment:

On Windows: llm_env\Scripts\activate

On macOS/Linux: source llm_env/bin/activate

Step 2: Install Framework Libraries

Next, install the LLM frameworks you've chosen. For example, if you are using PyTorch, you can install it by running:

pip install torch torchvision torchaudio

For TensorFlow, use the following:

```
pip install tensorflow
```

If you plan on using the Hugging Face Transformers library, which simplifies working with pre-trained models, install it by running:

```
pip install transformers
```

For GPU acceleration, make sure to install the appropriate CUDA versions along with the framework, particularly if you are working with large models that require high computational power.

Step 3: Verify Installations

After installation, verify that everything is set up correctly by running basic commands in Python:

For TensorFlow:

```
import tensorflow as tf

print(tf.__version__)
```

For PyTorch:

```
import torch

print(torch.__version__)
```

Ensure there are no errors, and that the framework versions are correctly displayed. This confirms that your environment is correctly configured.

- **Best Practices for Managing Dependencies**

- Use virtual environments: Always use virtual environments to avoid conflicts between project dependencies.

- Use dependency management tools: Tools like pip or conda are essential for managing and installing packages in Python projects. For team projects, include a requirements.txt file to track exact versions of libraries.

- Automate environment setup: Use scripts like Dockerfiles or environment management tools such as Docker to create reproducible environments, ensuring consistency across different machines and deployment platforms.

3.3 First Steps with LLM Models

Now that your environment is set up, you can begin experimenting with LLMs. The first step is to run a pre-trained model in your local environment to understand how LLMs work in practice.

Step 1: Load a Pre-Trained Model from Hugging Face

For a quick start, you can use the Hugging Face Transformers library to load a pre-trained LLM such as GPT-2. Below is an example using PyTorch:

1. Import the necessary libraries:

from transformers import GPT2LMHeadModel, GPT2Tokenizer

2. Load the pre-trained model and tokenizer:

```python
model = GPT2LMHeadModel.from_pretrained("gpt2")
tokenizer = GPT2Tokenizer.from_pretrained("gpt2")
```

3. Tokenize an input text and generate a response:

```python
input_text = "Hello, how are you?"
inputs = tokenizer.encode(input_text, return_tensors="pt")

outputs = model.generate(inputs, max_length=50, num_return_sequences=1)

generated_text = tokenizer.decode(outputs[0], skip_special_tokens=True)

print(generated_text)
```

This code loads the GPT-2 model, tokenizes a simple input phrase, and generates a continuation of that text. You can experiment with different inputs to see how the model generates responses.

Step 2: Customize Your Model for Specific Tasks

Once you have basic functionality working, you can start customizing your model for more specific tasks. For instance, you can fine-tune a model on your own dataset to make it more suitable for a particular domain or task. Fine-tuning typically involves:

1. Collecting domain-specific data.

2. Preprocessing the data (e.g., cleaning and tokenizing text).

3. Training the model on the custom dataset.

The Hugging Face library provides an easy-to-use Trainer API to facilitate this fine-tuning process.

Step 3: Monitor and Evaluate Performance

As you develop your model, it's important to evaluate its performance regularly. Common evaluation metrics for language models include perplexity and BLEU score. You can use the transformers library to load evaluation datasets and evaluate your model's performance. You can also monitor resource usage (memory, CPU/GPU load) to ensure that your local environment is optimized for the computational requirements of running LLMs.

By following these initial steps, you can effectively set up your development environment and start working with LLMs on your local machine. As you progress, you will continue to build upon these foundational steps, optimizing and tailoring your models for specific applications.

Chapter 4

Building Your First Local LLM

4.1 Selecting a Pre-trained Model

The process of selecting a pre-trained large language model (LLM) for local deployment begins with understanding your application's specific requirements. Different use cases demand different architectural and performance characteristics from a model. Key considerations include model size, memory footprint, domain alignment, licensing, inference speed, and community support.

● **Model Size and Resource Constraints**

Pre-trained models vary widely in size, from lightweight models with under 100 million parameters to expansive architectures like GPT-3 with over 175 billion parameters. For local deployment, especially on edge devices or consumer hardware, smaller models such as DistilBERT, TinyGPT, and LLaMA 2 7B are practical starting points. These models offer acceptable accuracy while remaining computationally efficient.

- Domain Alignment

Choosing a model that aligns with your application's domain improves accuracy and reduces the need for extensive fine-tuning. For instance, if building a legal document summarizer, models like Legal-BERT or CaseLaw-BERT are pre-trained on legal corpora. In contrast, general-purpose models like GPT-J or Falcon are trained on broader datasets and serve well in multi-domain applications.

- Licensing and Usage Restrictions

Open-source models such as LLaMA 2, BLOOM, and GPT-NeoX come with licenses that vary in permissiveness. It is essential to verify whether commercial use is allowed, especially if the application is intended for monetization. Models under the Apache 2.0 or MIT licenses generally offer fewer restrictions compared to those under research-only or non-commercial clauses.

- Community and Ecosystem Support

A strong developer community ensures better tooling, documentation, and community-driven improvements. Hugging Face Transformers hosts many models with active community engagement and robust APIs, simplifying integration and experimentation.

● **Understanding the Strengths and Weaknesses of Popular Models**

DistilBERT is a distilled version of BERT that offers faster performance and a smaller memory footprint. It is a good choice when latency and resource limitations are critical, but it might struggle with complex language understanding tasks. LLaMA 2 strikes a balance between size and performance, making it suitable for a wide range of tasks but requiring more hardware resources than smaller models. GPT-J is a powerful general-purpose model known for its open availability and strong language generation capabilities, but it demands substantial computational resources and is harder to run locally. Alpaca, which builds on LLaMA, has been fine-tuned for better instruction following, offering improved usability in conversational tasks, though its licensing may limit certain applications. BLOOM supports multiple languages and is completely open-source, but it is memory-intensive and less practical on consumer hardware.

Choosing the right model is a trade-off between performance, domain specificity, deployment feasibility, and legal usability. Profiling several candidates using test inputs can help narrow the selection.

4.2 Setting Up Local Deployment

Deploying a large language model locally involves environment setup, dependency management, hardware compatibility, and runtime orchestration. The goal is to run inference efficiently without relying on cloud infrastructure.

- **System Requirements and Hardware Considerations**

Most LLMs require a GPU for real-time or near-real-time performance, although CPU-only inference is possible with smaller models or with quantized versions. NVIDIA

GPUs with CUDA support are commonly used, along with software frameworks such as PyTorch or TensorFlow. For lighter deployments, tools like ONNX Runtime, GGML, or llama.cpp can run quantized models on CPU.

- Minimum recommended specifications:

RAM: 16 GB or more

GPU: 6 GB VRAM (for models up to 7B parameters)

CPU: Multi-core (8 cores or more preferred)

- Framework Installation

Set up begins with installing the appropriate libraries:

pip install torch torchvision torchaudio

pip install transformers accelerate

For quantized inference or CPU-only runs:

pip install optimum

Depending on the model, additional libraries like ggml, llama.cpp, or auto-gptq may be needed. Models downloaded from Hugging Face often include configuration files compatible with these frameworks.

- Model Download and Setup

Using Hugging Face Transformers:

from transformers import AutoModelForCausalLM, AutoTokenizer

```python
model_name = "meta-llama/Llama-2-7b-hf"

tokenizer                           =
AutoTokenizer.from_pretrained(model_na
me)

model                               =
AutoModelForCausalLM.from_pretrained(m
odel_name)
```

For llama.cpp:

```
git                              clone
https://github.com/ggerganov/llama.cpp

cd llama.cpp

make

./convert.py --model llama-2-7b
```

These tools enable conversion to CPU-optimized formats like INT4 or INT8.

Running Inference Locally

A simple inference example:

```
inputs = tokenizer("What is the capital of France?", return_tensors="pt")
outputs = model.generate(**inputs)
print(tokenizer.decode(outputs[0]))
```

App Integration

Integration into an application typically involves creating a REST API using frameworks such as FastAPI or Flask. This encapsulates the LLM and allows requests from frontend or other services.

Example using FastAPI:

```python
from fastapi import FastAPI, Request

from transformers import pipeline


app = FastAPI()

generator    =    pipeline("text-generation",
model=model, tokenizer=tokenizer)


@app.post("/generate")

async def generate(request: Request):

    data = await request.json()

    prompt = data.get("prompt")

    output    =    generator(prompt,
max_length=50)

    return    {"response":
output[0]["generated_text"]}
```

Deployment options include running the app via Uvicorn or Docker containers for consistent runtime environments.

4.3 Testing and Evaluating the Model

After local deployment, evaluating performance and correctness is essential. This ensures the model meets functional and non-functional requirements under realistic conditions.

Benchmarking Performance

Standard metrics include:

- Latency: Time taken to generate responses.

- Throughput: Number of inferences per second.

- Memory usage: Peak RAM and VRAM consumption.

- Token generation rate: Speed of output token creation (tokens/sec).

Tools like time, psutil, and nvtop can measure resource utilization. For more structured benchmarks, use lm-eval-harness or OpenLLM Leaderboard scripts. Example:

```
time python run_inference.py
```

- Evaluating Output Quality

For practical testing, use qualitative and quantitative methods:

BLEU, ROUGE, METEOR: Common NLP metrics for comparing generated text against references.

Task-specific evaluation: Classification accuracy, summarization fidelity, etc.

Human evaluation: Review by domain experts for coherence and relevance.

Testing across varied inputs reveals weaknesses in generation such as hallucination, ambiguity, or repetition. Logging responses helps identify patterns in output deficiencies.

Tuning Model Behavior

Several parameters affect output quality:

- Temperature: Controls randomness; lower values make output more deterministic.

- Top-k and top-p sampling: Restrict the token selection pool to improve relevance.

- Max tokens: Limits the output length.

Example configuration:

```
output = generator(

    prompt,

    max_length=100,

    temperature=0.7,

    top_k=50,

    top_p=0.95,

    do_sample=True )
```

Fine-tuning on a specific dataset may be required for sustained improvements. This can involve full fine-tuning or parameter-efficient methods like LoRA (Low-Rank Adaptation).

● **Monitoring and Iteration**

Local logging frameworks or Prometheus-based setups can monitor response times and system load in real-time. Collecting feedback from test users helps refine prompts and configuration settings. Continuous evaluation ensures the model remains aligned with evolving application needs.

Chapter 5

Customizing and Optimizing Local LLMs

5.1 Fine-Tuning LLMs for Specific Tasks

Fine-tuning allows a pre-trained large language model (LLM) to adapt to specific application needs by continuing the training process on a more targeted dataset. The general architecture of the model remains unchanged, but its weights are slightly adjusted to perform better on domain-specific tasks such as legal document parsing, medical question answering, or financial forecasting.

● **Techniques for Adaptation**

The most common fine-tuning approach is supervised fine-tuning (SFT). It involves training the model on labeled data where inputs are paired with expected outputs. For example, to build a customer support bot, a dataset of user queries and agent responses can be used. This technique aligns the model more closely with task-specific formats and language. Another method is instruction tuning, where the model is exposed to a variety of task instructions and learns to follow them. This approach improves generalization to new tasks that share structural similarities with the training tasks.

For efficiency, parameter-efficient fine-tuning (PEFT) methods such as Low-Rank Adaptation (LoRA), adapters, or prompt tuning can be employed. LoRA introduces additional trainable layers within the attention mechanism while keeping the base model frozen, significantly reducing the number of updated parameters. Adapters insert small neural modules between transformer layers, allowing for modular and reusable fine-tuning. Prompt tuning, instead of altering model weights, prepends learned embedding vectors (soft prompts) to the input.

• Domain-Specific Data Training

Performance gains in fine-tuning are directly tied to the quality and relevance of the dataset. For domain-specific tasks, it is essential to curate corpora that reflect the vocabulary, syntax, and semantics of the target domain. Preprocessing should ensure tokenization compatibility with the model's tokenizer, clean removal of noise, and normalization of terms.

During training, batch size, learning rate, and number of epochs must be chosen carefully to avoid overfitting. Evaluation should use task-specific metrics such as F1 score, accuracy, BLEU, or ROUGE, depending on the nature of the output.

Fine-tuning should be validated through ablation studies to understand the impact of training data size, input format, and model checkpoints. Tools such as Hugging Face's Trainer API or PyTorch Lightning simplify the training process by handling optimizers, schedulers, and checkpointing.

5.2 Optimizing Model Size for Local Deployment

Running LLMs on local hardware requires balancing performance with memory and compute constraints. Full-scale models like GPT-3 are not feasible for most consumer-grade devices. Instead, model size must be reduced while preserving task-relevant capabilities.

- **Reducing Model Size Without Accuracy Loss**

Smaller base models, such as DistilBERT, MobileBERT, and TinyLlama, are pre-trained to emulate the behavior of larger models through techniques like knowledge distillation. Distillation transfers the knowledge from a large "teacher" model to a compact "student" model by minimizing the divergence between their output distributions. This produces a lightweight model with competitive accuracy. Beyond selecting smaller architectures, one can apply post-training compression techniques. Weight pruning eliminates unnecessary connections in the model. Structured pruning removes entire heads, neurons, or layers that contribute minimally to final outputs, while unstructured pruning removes individual weights.

Quantization reduces the precision of model weights and activations. For example, 32-bit floating point values can be converted to 8-bit integers. Static quantization applies at inference time, while quantization-aware training (QAT) incorporates it during fine-tuning, preserving accuracy better in some scenarios.

Dynamic quantization only applies to activations during inference, striking a balance between performance gain and model fidelity. Quantized models not only reduce memory consumption but also accelerate computation on compatible hardware such as CPUs with AVX2/FMA or GPUs supporting INT8 operations.

● **Compression Toolkits and Libraries**

Several open-source libraries support model compression. ONNX Runtime, TensorRT, and OpenVINO offer quantization, pruning, and fusion optimizations for deployment. Hugging Face's Optimum and Intel's Neural Compressor enable easy integration of compression pipelines into the model training or inference workflow. Model checkpoint conversion from floating point to integer representation is critical. Care must be taken to preserve tokenizers, ensure compatibility with runtime environments, and verify that the post-compression model behaves identically on evaluation datasets.

Performance trade-offs should be monitored using profiling tools. Key metrics include model size, memory footprint, throughput (tokens/sec), and accuracy (on a fixed validation set).

5.3 Enhancing Performance

Local deployment demands that LLM-powered applications deliver low-latency responses without overwhelming system resources. This involves optimizing both inference speed and resource efficiency.

• Speed Optimizations for Local Apps

Model inference speed depends on multiple factors: model architecture, hardware acceleration, parallelism, and data loading. Transformer inference is bottlenecked by the attention mechanism, especially for long sequences. Efficient attention variants such as Linformer, Performer, or FlashAttention can replace standard attention layers to reduce computation from quadratic to linear or sub-quadratic complexity.

- Batching improves throughput but may introduce latency if not managed properly. Micro-batching, where multiple small requests are grouped within a strict time window, allows better utilization of compute units without long delays.

- Caching is another important technique. During autoregressive decoding, previously computed key-value pairs can be cached and reused, avoiding redundant computation. Libraries like Transformers and vLLM implement caching mechanisms out of the box.

- Quantized matrix operations, fused kernels, and operator optimization through libraries like TVM, XLA, and cuDNN can further reduce latency. Compiling models to low-level graph representations enables these toolchains to execute models closer to hardware.

● **Minimizing Latency and Computational Load**

Latency can also be reduced by simplifying model inputs. Limiting prompt length and avoiding unnecessary context tokens reduces the burden on the attention mechanism. Sequence truncation, summarization, or input reformulation are preprocessing strategies to achieve this.

Hardware-aware optimization plays a crucial role. Edge devices with GPU or NPU (Neural

Processing Unit) support can benefit from model partitioning, where parts of the computation are offloaded to different processors. This can be orchestrated using libraries like ONNX or frameworks like TensorFlow Lite.

Inference quantization should match hardware capabilities. For instance, Apple Silicon chips support 16-bit float (FP16) and INT8, while NVIDIA GPUs are optimal for mixed-precision inference with Tensor Cores. Choosing the correct precision level ensures minimal trade-off between speed and quality.

Multithreading and asynchronous execution allow better CPU utilization. For example, serving multiple users can be achieved with thread pools or coroutine-based concurrency in Python using frameworks like FastAPI or asyncio.

Finally, model loading strategies such as lazy loading (loading only required weights) or memory mapping (accessing weights directly from disk) conserve memory and speed up initialization, particularly on devices with limited RAM.

In combination, fine-tuning, compression, and performance optimizations allow developers to deploy local LLMs that are capable, responsive, and efficient. These techniques transform resource-intensive models into practical tools for real-time, domain-specific applications on local systems.

Chapter 6

Integrating LLMs into Real-World
Applications

6.1 Building Intelligent User Interfaces

- Designing Conversational UIs with LLMs

Large Language Models (LLMs) have changed how users interact with software. They enable conversational interfaces that understand natural language and respond contextually. Designing a user interface (UI) for LLM-based applications requires a shift from static forms and buttons to fluid interactions where language becomes the primary input.

In a conversational UI, the model's output must be context-aware and coherent across multi-turn dialogues. This demands managing conversation state, memory, and context persistence. Developers often use token-based memory management to maintain conversational continuity while staying within the model's token limit. For example, frameworks like LangChain or llamaindex can help manage context windows and memory buffers when building local LLM-powered UIs.

The front-end interface should be designed to accommodate both free-text input and guided interaction. Input components can include text fields with autocomplete, dropdowns for structured prompts, and even buttons for quick replies to steer the conversation. On the back end, prompt engineering remains a critical part of the design, ensuring that inputs are structured to elicit useful and safe responses. Latency is a key consideration. Local LLMs typically run on constrained hardware compared to cloud solutions. Efficient inference, caching, and batching can significantly reduce perceived lag in conversational interfaces. Developers may use optimized libraries like llama.cpp, ggml, or ONNX runtime for faster model inference on CPUs and GPUs.

● **Voice Input/Output Integration**

Voice interfaces require two core capabilities: automatic speech recognition (ASR) and text-to-speech (TTS). Integrating these with a local LLM enables natural, hands-free interaction. For ASR, open-source libraries like Vosk or Whisper (fine-tuned for edge devices) can convert speech to text efficiently. Whisper.cpp is a popular lightweight adaptation for local deployment.

For TTS, engines like Coqui TTS, Mozilla TTS, or eSpeak NG allow text responses to be spoken back to the user. These components can be containerized or embedded in desktop/mobile applications alongside the LLM.

To ensure a seamless experience, audio processing should be handled asynchronously. A separate thread or worker process can manage voice input/output without blocking the UI or model inference pipeline. Developers must also implement error handling for voice recognition accuracy, especially in noisy environments.

Proper UX design includes fallback options, like showing the transcribed text before confirmation or providing a retry mechanism. This helps users stay in control even if voice processing encounters issues. In safety-critical applications, voice commands should trigger confirmation prompts before executing actions.

6.2 Advanced Features for Smart Apps

- Real-time Data Processing with Local LLMs

Unlike cloud-based models, local LLMs can be tightly coupled with edge data sources such as sensors, logs, and internal APIs. This enables real-time processing where the model responds to data as it arrives, without relying on remote calls. This is particularly valuable in IoT environments, on-prem systems, or disconnected networks. For example, an industrial monitoring app could use a local LLM to interpret error logs in real-time, explain anomalies in natural language, and suggest corrective actions. This requires streaming data pipelines that feed structured data into the model as contextual information. Libraries like Apache Kafka, Redis Streams, or even lightweight in-memory queues can serve as the data bridge.

Prompt construction becomes dynamic. Inputs to the LLM can be formatted with the latest data points, and the response can be used to trigger alerts, populate dashboards, or interact with other system components. Because latency and bandwidth are minimized with local deployment, feedback loops become more responsive.

In scenarios where the data volume is high, pre-processing or summarization steps can reduce input size before sending it to the LLM. Developers can use rules-based systems or smaller neural models upstream to select relevant data. This hybrid approach conserves resources while maintaining intelligent behavior.

- **Contextual and Personalized Responses in Apps**

Personalization is one of the core strengths of integrating LLMs in local applications. Unlike cloud APIs that abstract user data for privacy, local models can access and process user-specific information without external exposure. This enables more contextual and secure personalization. User preferences, recent interactions, device usage patterns, and stored data can be included in prompts or embeddings to guide the LLM's behavior. For example, a productivity app might tailor suggestions based on the user's calendar, notes, or recent tasks. This requires building a local context manager that retrieves and formats relevant data on-the-fly.

Embedding models, like sentence-transformers, can be used to semantically encode user history and search it efficiently via vector databases like FAISS or Chroma. This enhances contextual relevance without requiring full prompt history. Local RAG (retrieval-augmented generation) pipelines can enable semantic search and intelligent Q&A within app-specific knowledge bases. Privacy-aware design is essential. While storing user data locally avoids external transmission, developers must still secure it through encryption, access controls, and data expiration policies. Contextual features should degrade gracefully if the data is unavailable, ensuring a robust fallback mechanism.

6.3 Best Practices for Local LLM App Design

- Designing Apps That Work Seamlessly with LLMs

- Successful integration of LLMs requires thinking beyond just running a model locally. The entire application architecture must be aligned to support the LLM's requirements, resource consumption, and interaction patterns.

- Apps should adopt modular design principles. The LLM inference engine, data sources, UI components, and context manager should operate as decoupled services. This makes the system easier to maintain and scale. For instance, message queues or publish-subscribe systems can manage communication between components.

- Model lifecycle management is another critical factor. Developers need to handle model loading, caching, updates, and memory cleanup effectively. Hot-swapping models or running multiple variants (e.g., a small model for fast interactions and a large model for detailed tasks) may be appropriate in some cases. Frameworks like Ollama or GPT4All simplify model orchestration for local deployments.

- Consistency in prompt engineering is key. Inputs should follow a controlled template or pattern to reduce unexpected outputs. Additionally, UI components should include feedback loops allowing users to rate, correct, or flag model responses. These inputs can inform future prompt refinements or fine-tuning datasets.

- Fail-safe mechanisms must be integrated throughout the app. This includes setting token limits, managing output length, validating model responses before acting on them, and having fallbacks when the model fails or returns null. Designing for graceful degradation ensures the app remains functional even under constrained conditions.

● **Ensuring a User-Friendly Experience**

User experience design must bridge the gap between technical capabilities and human expectations. Since LLMs are probabilistic and may produce inconsistent outputs, the interface should guide users through predictable and controlled interactions.

Clear instructions, suggestions, and contextual hints can help users frame their queries effectively. Autocomplete, grammar checks, or prompt templates can improve input quality, which directly affects model performance. Visual indicators such as loading spinners or confidence bars can manage user expectations about response time and reliability.

Accessibility features are also important. This includes screen reader support, voice navigation, adjustable text sizes, and multilingual capabilities. LLMs can enhance accessibility by summarizing content, simplifying language, or translating interfaces on-the-fly. These features should be carefully tested to ensure reliability.

Local deployment poses specific challenges for UX: devices may have limited resources, power constraints, or varying screen sizes. Adaptive design principles, offline fallback logic, and user-controlled settings for performance vs. quality tradeoffs are essential.

Finally, transparency builds trust. The app should communicate when a model is generating a response, and offer an explanation feature if the output is complex. Users should be able to inspect the reasoning or data sources behind the answer, especially in domains like healthcare, law, or finance. Combining LLMs with rule-based logic for critical operations ensures both innovation and accountability.

Chapter 7

Ensuring Data Privacy and Security

7.1 Local Data Processing Benefits

The architecture of large language models (LLMs) traditionally leans toward centralized cloud-based services. However, this approach raises immediate concerns regarding data privacy, latency, and compliance. The shift toward local deployment of LLMs is driven by the demand for more secure, controllable, and privacy-preserving AI systems. Local data processing offers several practical advantages for developers building privacy-conscious applications.

● **Enhanced Data Sovereignty**

Running LLMs locally ensures that sensitive data never leaves the device or controlled network environment. In contrast to cloud-based LLMs, which require users to send inputs to remote servers, local models process information in situ. This design grants complete control over user data, reducing the exposure surface and eliminating reliance on third-party infrastructure.

Data sovereignty is critical in domains such as healthcare, legal, and finance, where client or patient data cannot legally be transferred across borders or stored in external data centers. Local models help developers meet these stringent requirements without sacrificing the capabilities of advanced natural language processing.

- Minimized Risk of Interception and Leakage

Every time data is transmitted over a network—whether encrypted or not—it introduces risk. Attackers can exploit vulnerabilities in transit layers, intercept packets, or compromise backend servers. With local LLMs, input and output stay within the execution environment, eliminating most network-related threat vectors.

This approach prevents accidental data leaks that could occur from misconfigured APIs, insecure webhooks, or unauthorized third-party services. For highly sensitive applications, such as legal assistants or on-device personal health advisors, local inference is not just preferable—it's essential.

- Improved Latency and Offline Availability

Although not a privacy concern in itself, reduced latency contributes to a better user experience and supports privacy by avoiding external dependencies. Applications that function entirely offline also ensure users retain access to services without uploading any data externally. This is especially beneficial in regions with limited connectivity or in cases where users are explicitly concerned about data traceability.

7.2 Security Measures for Local LLM Apps

Local deployment removes cloud-specific attack surfaces, but it doesn't eliminate the need for rigorous security practices. Once a model is integrated into an application, it becomes part of the attack surface. Ensuring that local LLM-powered applications remain secure requires a combination of system-level protections, encryption, secure architecture, and application-layer controls.

• Data Encryption at Rest and In Use

All sensitive data that interacts with the model—whether it's training data, runtime inputs, or logs—should be encrypted. Encryption at rest protects data stored on the device or server, while encryption in use (including in-memory encryption) ensures protection during computation.

Full-disk encryption (e.g., using LUKS or BitLocker) is a baseline. For app-specific storage, implement field-level encryption using industry-standard libraries such as libsodium or AES-GCM. Runtime memory should be cleared of sensitive data immediately after inference to minimize the window for memory scraping attacks.

In advanced implementations, developers can consider homomorphic encryption or trusted execution environments (TEEs) for scenarios where processing sensitive inputs must be isolated and provably secure. While these methods come with computational costs, they offer higher levels of data assurance.

● **Model Access Control and Isolation**

The LLM instance must be sandboxed to prevent unauthorized access from other processes or users on the same device. Containerization (e.g., via Docker or Podman), combined with minimal privilege principles, ensures that even if one component is compromised, it doesn't result in full system exposure.

For mobile applications, models can be deployed inside secure app sandboxes using OS-level isolation mechanisms (e.g., iOS App Sandbox, Android SELinux). For desktop and edge devices, consider using user-level namespaces and systemd protections to run inference services with reduced permissions.

Model access should also be gated behind authentication mechanisms if exposed through a local API. Even on localhost, unauthorized software or malware may attempt to interact with an unprotected endpoint.

● **Secure Model Update Mechanisms**

Local LLMs, like any software component, may require periodic updates to patch vulnerabilities or improve performance. Secure update mechanisms are necessary to prevent tampering or injection of malicious payloads.

Digital signing of update packages using GPG or similar schemes ensures the authenticity and integrity of model binaries. Implementing checksums and signature verification prior to applying updates can thwart supply chain attacks. Furthermore, updates should be fetched over encrypted channels (e.g., HTTPS with certificate pinning).

Avoid over-the-air updates in sensitive deployments unless strictly necessary. If OTA is required, provide users with explicit control and transparency over what is being downloaded and installed.

● **Input Sanitization and Output Monitoring**

Although LLMs are robust in handling natural language, they can still be exploited through prompt injection or adversarial inputs. Local applications must implement input sanitization layers to block malformed or potentially harmful instructions.

Output monitoring is equally important. Responses from the model should be filtered or constrained to prevent unintended disclosure of sensitive information, hallucinated facts, or unsafe actions. When possible, wrap LLM outputs with rule-based validation to ensure conformity to domain-specific constraints.

7.3 Compliance with Data Regulations

Developers working with local LLMs are not exempt from regulatory requirements. While local processing reduces the risk profile and simplifies many compliance concerns, adherence to privacy laws such as the General Data Protection Regulation (GDPR) and California Consumer Privacy Act (CCPA) still applies.

● **GDPR and Local LLMs**

Under GDPR, data controllers must ensure lawful, fair, and transparent processing of personal data. When deploying LLMs locally, developers must consider several core principles:

- Data Minimization: Collect and process only what is necessary. Inputs to the LLM should be relevant and limited to the task at hand.

- Purpose Limitation: Use the data only for the stated purpose. LLM-based applications must clearly communicate how user data is processed and used.

- User Rights: Ensure that users can access, correct, or delete their personal data. Even if processing is local, applications should allow users to manage their data footprints within the app.

- Security by Design: Local deployment inherently supports this, but developers must still demonstrate that technical safeguards are in place.

GDPR Article 25 emphasizes "data protection by design and by default." Local LLM apps align with this principle by processing information directly on the device, avoiding unnecessary transfers or retention.

However, if the app logs input or output data, even for debugging, these logs must be managed carefully and possibly anonymized. Developers should also provide a clear privacy policy and ensure that any data retained is encrypted and deletable on request.

● **CCPA Compliance Considerations**

CCPA focuses on consumer rights around the collection and sale of personal data. Even if no external server is involved, a local app must provide:

-Notice at Collection: Inform users about what personal data is being processed, even if it's not leaving the device.

- Right to Delete: Allow users to clear any stored interaction history or related metadata.

- No Sale Assurance: Clearly indicate that user data is not being sold or shared. Local LLMs are well-positioned here, but transparency still matters.

- Reasonable Security: Apply robust measures to safeguard user information from unauthorized access or theft.

CCPA has specific enforcement triggers based on the size and scope of business. Developers creating consumer-facing apps should assess whether their deployment falls within the legal thresholds and be prepared to comply accordingly.

● **Implementation Practices for Regulatory Compliance**

To support ongoing compliance, local LLM app developers should:

1. Maintain internal documentation about data flows, model behavior, and data access controls.

2. Conduct regular audits of model usage patterns and ensure that logs or stored results do not inadvertently retain identifiable information.

3. Use privacy-enhancing technologies like differential privacy or synthetic data when generating logs or metrics.

4. Implement modular data retention policies within the application, allowing users and administrators to specify what data is stored and for how long.

Consent management frameworks can also be embedded within the app interface, giving users control over personalization features, data usage, and analytics preferences.

Chapter 8

Troubleshooting and Debugging LLM Apps

8.1 Common Issues in LLM Engineering

Building local applications powered by Large Language Models (LLMs) presents distinct engineering challenges. Unlike conventional software, LLM behavior is probabilistic, meaning that bugs are not always reproducible, and performance issues can be influenced by data, hardware limitations, and model architecture. Developers must consider both software-level bugs and model-level misbehavior.

● Memory Errors

Memory consumption is one of the most frequent obstacles when deploying LLMs locally. Most modern LLMs require substantial RAM and GPU memory, even for inference. Memory issues typically manifest in the following forms:

- Out of Memory (OOM) Errors: These occur when the model, during loading or inference, exceeds available system or GPU memory. This is common when using models with billions of parameters.

- Fragmentation: On long-running applications, memory fragmentation can reduce the amount of usable memory even if total free memory appears sufficient.

- Memory Leaks: These arise when model-related objects (like tokenizers, tensors, or sessions) are not properly garbage collected or deallocated, especially when integrating models in multi-threaded environments.

- **Mitigation Strategies:**

- Use optimized and quantized versions of models (e.g., 8-bit or 4-bit variants).

- Implement efficient batching strategies and limit the input sequence length.

- Regularly profile memory usage using tools like tracemalloc (Python), NVIDIA's NSight, or PyTorch's memory profiler.

- Explicitly release memory using torch.cuda.empty_cache() and gc.collect() after inference.

- **Performance Bottlenecks**

Performance problems can appear as slow response times, unresponsive UIs, or system lag. The primary causes include:

- Excessive Latency: Caused by long sequence lengths, suboptimal model architectures, or insufficient hardware acceleration.

- CPU/GPU Saturation: LLM inference can fully utilize available compute resources, degrading overall system responsiveness.

- Inefficient Data Handling: Poor pre-processing and I/O operations can add overhead that compounds inference time.

● **Optimization Techniques:**

- Use model variants like DistilGPT or TinyBERT for lightweight deployments.

- Cache tokenized inputs when possible to reduce preprocessing overhead.

- Implement asynchronous processing or background threads to prevent blocking the main app flow.

- Use ONNX Runtime or TensorRT for inference acceleration.

● **Debugging Strategies**

Debugging LLM applications involves a combination of traditional software debugging and model-centric diagnostics. Key approaches include:

- Reproducibility: Set random seeds (e.g., torch.manual_seed) during debugging to ensure consistent model outputs.

- Instrumentation: Integrate logging at key points—input tokenization, model inference, response generation—to isolate performance and output issues.

- Unit Testing of Pre/Post-processing Pipelines: Ensure consistent and correct text cleaning, tokenization, and decoding routines.

- Profiling: Use profiling tools (e.g., cProfile, Py-Spy, PyTorch Profiler) to analyze performance hotspots.

- Monitoring GPU Metrics: Continuously monitor GPU usage, temperature, and power consumption using nvidia-smi or NVML bindings.

8.2 Handling Model Inaccuracies

Local LLMs often produce inaccurate, irrelevant, or contextually inappropriate outputs. Unlike rule-based systems, the variability of LLM responses makes debugging and correction more complex.

● **Identifying Flawed Outputs**

Model inaccuracies usually fall into several patterns:

- Hallucination: The model generates plausible-sounding but incorrect or fabricated content.

- Context Misalignment: The model misinterprets user input, especially if it's ambiguous or multi-intent.

- Bias and Toxicity: Models can produce outputs that reflect undesirable biases from their training data.

- Repetition or Truncation: Incomplete outputs or excessive looping in text generation due to sampling issues.

● **Detection Approaches:**

- Log model responses alongside input prompts and track anomalies manually or through heuristics.

- Build automated quality evaluation tools using BLEU, ROUGE, or embedding similarity scores.

- Implement sanity checks (e.g., regex-based validations) for domain-specific constraints (like dates, names, product codes).

● **Corrective Measures**

- Prompt Engineering: The fastest intervention is improving the prompt structure. Adding explicit instructions, providing examples, or formatting inputs can guide the model more effectively.

- Few-shot Learning: Including example Q&A pairs in the input can help condition the model toward accurate responses.

- Post-processing Filters: Apply domain-specific logic to verify or correct model outputs after generation.

- Confidence Estimation: Use entropy of the output probability distribution to estimate uncertainty and flag low-confidence responses.

• Fine-tuning for Accuracy and Relevance

Fine-tuning is essential when the application domain requires specialized knowledge or behavior. Steps include:

- Curating Domain-Specific Datasets: Use text data reflective of the desired language style, terminology, and structure.

- Choosing the Right Objective: Use supervised fine-tuning with cross-entropy loss for classification and generation tasks.

- Evaluation and Feedback Loop: Use a hold-out validation set and track metrics like perplexity, accuracy, or F1 score. Integrate user feedback to iteratively improve performance.

- Regularization and Overfitting Prevention: Apply dropout, data augmentation, or early stopping during training to improve generalization.

8.3 Testing for Robustness

Robustness ensures that an LLM-powered application behaves consistently across a wide range of inputs and usage conditions. This is crucial for production environments where edge cases and unpredictable user behavior are inevitable.

● **Stress Testing Techniques**

Stress testing aims to identify failure points by pushing the system beyond its normal operating conditions.

- Input Size Limits: Test with maximum token limits to see if the system fails gracefully.

- Concurrent Requests: Simulate multiple parallel inference requests to measure scalability.

- Resource Exhaustion: Gradually increase memory or CPU usage and observe system stability under constrained resources.

- Random and Noisy Inputs: Feed gibberish, out-of-domain inputs, or malformed queries to test system robustness and crash resistance.

Use frameworks like Locust, Artillery, or custom scripts with Python's asyncio and multiprocessing for generating load and tracking behavior.

● **Handling Edge Cases**

Edge cases are user inputs that are rare or difficult to interpret. Examples include:

- Mixed language inputs

- Idiomatic or colloquial phrases

- Contradictory or vague questions

● **Defensive Programming Approaches:**

- Implement input validation layers to sanitize or reject ambiguous queries.

- Use fallback rules or default responses when the model output fails validation.

- Provide users with clarification questions when input is incomplete or ambiguous.

● **Ensuring Stability Across Versions**

As models or codebases are updated, regression testing is essential to prevent previously resolved issues from resurfacing.

- Version Control of Models: Store each fine-tuned model version with metadata including training data, parameters, and performance benchmarks.

- Snapshot Testing: Save output samples for key input prompts and re-test them across versions to ensure consistency.

- Automated Test Suites: Implement CI pipelines that automatically run performance, accuracy, and reliability tests whenever code or model updates are made.

This chapter has outlined the core challenges in debugging and ensuring stability in LLM-based applications. Practical tools and strategies have been discussed to address memory and performance issues, improve model accuracy, and conduct thorough robustness testing. These practices are fundamental for deploying reliable and efficient local LLM solutions in production environments.

Chapter 9

Scaling Local LLM Solutions

9.1 Strategies for Scaling Local Models

Scaling a locally deployed Large Language Model (LLM) requires careful planning across three dimensions: performance, resource utilization, and adaptability to real-world demands. Unlike cloud-based systems that can rely on elastic infrastructure, local deployments are constrained by the host system's hardware. Effective scaling strategies aim to maximize performance while maintaining responsiveness and efficient memory and compute usage.

● **When to Scale**

Identifying the right time to scale a local LLM involves monitoring system bottlenecks and user behavior. Indicators include:

- Latency Increases: If response times increase under moderate load, the model may be saturating CPU or GPU resources.

- Resource Saturation: Frequent CPU spikes, GPU overutilization, or memory exhaustion suggest the current setup is not sustainable.

- User Growth: A consistent increase in active users, sessions, or concurrent queries indicates the need to scale.

Scaling should be considered when these signs are persistent and affect the quality of user interaction or model accuracy.

● **Vertical Scaling**

Vertical scaling refers to upgrading the hardware of a single device to support larger or faster models. Key tactics include:

- High-End GPUs: Employing GPUs with larger VRAM (e.g., 24GB or more) enables running larger models like LLaMA or Falcon variants locally.

- RAM Expansion: Increasing system RAM ensures smoother data loading and reduces reliance on slow disk I/O.

- SSD Utilization: Faster SSDs reduce bottlenecks in model loading and data retrieval.

This method is suitable when the deployment is limited to a single device or a compact system like an embedded device or edge server.

● **Horizontal Scaling**

For broader scalability, horizontal scaling distributes workloads across multiple devices. This involves:

- Model Sharding: Splitting a model across several devices where each handles part of the computation. Frameworks like DeepSpeed or Megatron-LM enable such setups.

- Load Balancing: Distributing incoming queries among multiple instances of a model running on different machines or containers. Tools like Docker Swarm, Kubernetes, or even simple round-robin algorithms can help.

- Edge Collaboration: In decentralized deployments, devices at the edge collaborate by sharing portions of the model or processing pipeline.

Horizontal scaling allows for parallelization and redundancy but increases complexity in synchronization and latency control.

● **Quantization and Pruning**

Scaling locally also involves optimizing model architecture and weights. Quantization reduces the precision of weights from FP32 to INT8 or lower, significantly reducing model size and memory requirements. Techniques include:

- Post-Training Quantization (PTQ)

- Quantization-Aware Training (QAT)

Pruning removes less significant neurons or layers in the model, trading minimal accuracy for improved speed and lower resource use. Both techniques can enable deployment of more capable models on limited hardware.

● **Model Distillation**

Another method is distillation, where a smaller model (student) is trained to mimic a larger model (teacher). This results in lighter models suitable for low-power devices without substantial loss in capability. Distilled models such as DistilBERT or TinyGPT offer solid performance with a reduced computational footprint.

9.2 Handling Increased User Demand

As user demand grows, performance degradation becomes a significant concern. Addressing increased load requires architectural and algorithmic strategies that maintain throughput, reliability, and responsiveness.

● **Concurrency Management**

Handling simultaneous queries efficiently is crucial. This is typically managed via:

- Thread Pools and Async Processing: Languages like Python (asyncio) or Rust (Tokio) allow non-blocking calls that improve responsiveness.

- Model Batching: Combining multiple input queries into a single batch reduces overhead and improves GPU throughput.

- Queue Systems: Systems like RabbitMQ or Redis queues can throttle and prioritize user requests to prevent server overload.

● **Resource Allocation**

Proper allocation of computational resources improves resilience to spikes in usage:

- CPU/GPU Affinity: Pinning processes to specific cores or GPU threads prevents resource contention.

- Memory Limits: Applying limits prevents rogue queries or large payloads from crashing the system.

- Caching Mechanisms: Reusing responses for frequently asked queries reduces redundant computations. Libraries like Faiss can accelerate semantic similarity searches.

● **Distributed Inference**

For substantial demand, distributed inference is essential. This involves splitting the inference pipeline across multiple nodes:

- Tensor Parallelism: Distributes tensor operations across GPUs or nodes.

- Pipeline Parallelism: Each model layer or group of layers runs on a different node, passing intermediate results downstream.

Both techniques are supported in frameworks like Hugging Face Accelerate and NVIDIA Triton. For edge deployments, lightweight orchestration tools can manage multiple Raspberry Pi or Jetson Nano devices acting as a distributed inference cluster.

● **Dynamic Scaling Policies**

Implementing auto-scaling policies that respond to demand spikes can prevent service interruptions:

- Monitoring Tools: Prometheus, Grafana, or Telegraf collect system metrics and help predict scaling triggers.

- Policy Engines: Custom scripts or open-source platforms like KEDA (Kubernetes Event-driven Autoscaling) can automate the scaling process based on CPU usage, query frequency, or memory usage.

9.3 Optimizing for Cross-Platform Deployment

Ensuring a local LLM application runs effectively across diverse platforms—mobile, desktop, and web—requires architecture flexibility and consistent performance tuning.

● **Platform Abstraction**

Building platform-independent applications starts with abstracting hardware and OS dependencies:

- Containerization: Tools like Docker encapsulate applications with all dependencies, ensuring consistent behavior across environments.

- Cross-Compilers and Toolchains: Use of cross-platform compilers such as LLVM or build tools like CMake helps target different operating systems from a single codebase.

- Hardware Abstraction Layers (HALs): Especially in embedded and mobile environments, HALs provide a uniform interface to the underlying hardware, simplifying deployment.

● **Language and Framework Choices**

Selecting technologies that support cross-platform compatibility is crucial:

- Mobile: TensorFlow Lite and ONNX Runtime Mobile allow running quantized models on Android or iOS with minimal resource usage.

- Desktop: PyTorch, ONNX Runtime, and Hugging Face Transformers run effectively on most desktops with sufficient memory and GPU.

- Web: WebAssembly (WASM) and TensorFlow.js enable LLMs to run in browsers. Though limited in model size, these are suitable for lightweight applications and real-time interactivity.

Framework wrappers like TFLite's delegates (GPU, NNAPI) or ONNX's EPs (Execution Providers) adapt inference to the target hardware for optimal performance.

● **UI and UX Considerations**

Different platforms require different interaction paradigms. A few considerations include:

- Responsiveness: Mobile users expect near-instant feedback, requiring lightweight models and low-latency processing.

- Resource Awareness: Background inference tasks must adapt to battery and thermal constraints on mobile devices.

- Modular UI: Designing modular user interfaces allows reusability across platforms, using frameworks like Flutter or React Native.

● **Synchronization and State Management**

When deploying across platforms, shared state and synchronized logic are critical:

- Local Caching: To ensure continuity, cache recent interactions locally with version control for updates.

- Sync Protocols: Use lightweight sync mechanisms (e.g., MQTT, WebSockets) for cross-device state sharing.

- Unified Storage Formats: Use portable formats like JSON, Protocol Buffers, or SQLite to ensure consistency in data representation.

● **Testing and Debugging**

Robust cross-platform testing ensures stability:

- Automated Testing: Use CI/CD tools that run unit and integration tests across platforms (GitHub Actions, Bitrise).

- Emulation and Simulation: Test applications on emulators/simulators with varying hardware profiles to detect bottlenecks and edge-case failures.

The variability of local environments demands thorough profiling on each platform. Profilers like Android Studio, Xcode Instruments, and Visual Studio Diagnostic Tools are essential for fine-tuning app behavior.

Scaling local LLM solutions requires deliberate architecture planning, hardware-aware optimization, and resilient cross-platform design. Each strategy contributes to maintaining a responsive and adaptable user experience as usage grows and environments diversify.

Chapter 10

The Future of LLM Engineering and Smart Applications

10.1 Emerging Trends in LLM Engineering

Large Language Models (LLMs) have evolved from research prototypes to practical tools in production environments. Recent years have shown that this field moves rapidly, with constant improvements in performance, efficiency, and accessibility. Engineers working in this space need to stay updated with emerging architectural shifts, deployment strategies, and optimization techniques to maintain relevance and effectiveness.

• Advancements in Model Architectures

The transformer architecture remains the backbone of most LLMs, but modifications are continuously introduced to address key limitations—particularly in terms of latency, memory usage, and scalability. Sparse transformers and Mixture of Experts (MoE) models have gained attention for their ability to scale model capacity without linear increases in computational cost. Sparse attention mechanisms reduce the quadratic complexity of standard attention by selectively attending to relevant tokens. This change improves inference speed, particularly for long-sequence tasks. Models like Longformer and BigBird are optimized for scenarios involving long documents or sessions, such as chat histories or legal texts.

MoE models, such as GLaM and Switch Transformer, distribute computation across multiple expert subnetworks, only activating a subset during each forward pass. This leads to high parameter counts with reduced active computation per request.

This architecture provides high performance while conserving compute resources. Another area of interest is modular and compositional models. Instead of monolithic LLMs, modular systems use multiple specialized models working in tandem. For example, one model may handle language understanding, another may handle context retention, and another might specialize in task-specific logic. This approach enhances flexibility, maintainability, and interpretability.

● **Quantization, Pruning, and Distillation**

Deploying models locally requires optimization strategies that reduce size and improve inference speed without significant loss in accuracy. Quantization reduces the precision of weights and activations— commonly from float32 to int8 or even 4-bit formats—resulting in smaller models and faster matrix operations. Libraries like bitsandbytes, Intel Neural Compressor, and TensorRT support mixed-precision inference pipelines tailored for local deployment.

Pruning eliminates redundant or less impactful weights in a neural network. Structural pruning removes entire neurons or attention heads, while unstructured pruning zeroes out individual weights. Pruned models can often retain up to 90% of their performance while shrinking significantly in size.

Knowledge distillation is another effective approach. A smaller model (the student) is trained to emulate a larger one (the teacher), preserving functionality while requiring less memory and compute. Distilled models like DistilBERT and TinyGPT are widely used in mobile and embedded systems.

● On-Device Training and Edge Adaptation

Traditionally, training has been confined to centralized data centers due to the need for large-scale compute. However, advancements in model efficiency and hardware accelerators have enabled a form of training on consumer-grade devices. Techniques such as Low-Rank Adaptation (LoRA) and Parameter-Efficient Fine-Tuning (PEFT) allow selective tuning of small parameter subsets. These techniques enable rapid task adaptation on-device with minimal memory overhead. Edge devices, including smartphones and IoT units with NPUs, are now capable of running compressed versions of LLMs locally. Apple's Core ML and Qualcomm's AI Engine support native model execution with high energy efficiency. These developments allow for real-time LLM inference without relying on network connectivity or cloud resources.

10.2 Opportunities in Various Industries

The shift from cloud-based AI to locally deployed, efficient models has opened practical applications across diverse industries. Beyond reducing dependency on remote servers, local LLMs enable real-time performance, greater data control, and cost-efficient scalability.

● **Healthcare**

In clinical settings, local LLMs can support diagnostics, documentation, and real-time translation with strict data privacy. Since patient data is sensitive and subject to regulatory frameworks like HIPAA and GDPR, keeping LLMs on-premise or embedded in secure hospital networks ensures compliance and security. Medical transcription and decision support systems powered by LLMs help reduce administrative burdens. Models trained on domain-specific vocabularies can summarize patient records, suggest ICD-10 codes, and flag potential contraindications in prescriptions. For example, a local model embedded in a radiology suite can generate report drafts while maintaining offline operation.

● **Finance**

Financial institutions benefit from LLMs for automating document analysis, risk modeling, and fraud detection. Given the sensitivity of customer data, local processing reduces exposure to external breaches. Local LLMs can parse financial documents, extract key performance indicators, and assist analysts in generating summaries or forecasts. In algorithmic trading, latency is critical. Running LLMs directly on trading systems ensures faster decision cycles. Furthermore, fine-tuned LLMs can monitor regulatory updates, perform sentiment analysis on news feeds, and assess compliance risks without uploading confidential data to cloud services.

● **Customer Service and CRM**

Local LLMs enable responsive, intelligent customer support interfaces with enhanced privacy and personalization. These models can operate inside point-of-sale systems, kiosks, or mobile apps, responding to customer queries, suggesting products, or assisting with troubleshooting without relying on external servers.

In customer relationship management (CRM), LLMs help generate context-aware responses based on user profiles, past interactions, and preferences. These capabilities support better engagement while preserving user trust. For industries like banking or insurance, keeping interactions local aligns with internal risk policies and builds transparency.

● **Manufacturing and Logistics**

Factories and supply chains use LLMs for predictive maintenance, anomaly detection, and multilingual operator interfaces. These applications often require real-time response in bandwidth-constrained environments. Deploying optimized models locally avoids the delays and instability of remote inference. In logistics, LLMs assist with route optimization, report generation, and document classification, improving operational efficiency. Local execution is especially useful in remote or mobile environments where connectivity cannot be guaranteed.

● **Education and Research**

LLMs have become integral in personalized education platforms. They can tutor, explain, and quiz users based on their pace and learning style. Local deployment is key in institutions with limited or restricted internet access. Additionally, LLMs can operate as research assistants, parsing datasets, summarizing findings, and generating code or documentation— valuable in academia and labs with strict data-sharing policies.

10.3 Building a Career in LLM Engineering

The rising demand for LLM-powered applications has created a niche yet rapidly expanding career path. LLM engineers are expected to bridge the gap between machine learning research, software development, and domain-specific applications.

- **Core Skills**

A solid foundation in computer science and software engineering is essential. Familiarity with Python and frameworks such as PyTorch, TensorFlow, and Hugging Face Transformers is a baseline requirement. Understanding of data structures, algorithms, and software architecture supports the integration of models into complex systems. Proficiency in deep learning theory—especially the mechanics of attention, gradient descent, and optimization algorithms—enables fine-tuning and debugging. Engineers must also understand GPU acceleration, CUDA programming, and low-level optimizations for running models efficiently. Knowledge of quantization techniques, model compression, and tools like ONNX, TensorRT, or OpenVINO is increasingly important. These allow for converting and optimizing models for deployment across different hardware targets.

For those working with on-device or embedded deployments, familiarity with mobile development environments (Android NNAPI, Apple Core ML, etc.) and hardware inference SDKs is valuable.

● **Practical Experience and Projects**

Hands-on experience with real datasets, training routines, and inference pipelines distinguishes candidates in this field. Building applications that demonstrate practical uses of LLMs—such as document summarizers, chatbots, code assistants, or transcription tools—helps showcase applied skills. Participating in open-source projects, contributing to libraries like transformers or llama.cpp, or building wrapper libraries for inference can further build credibility. Competitions like Hugging Face Challenges or Kaggle NLP competitions offer opportunities to benchmark skills against real-world problems.

● **Learning Resources**

Ongoing learning is critical due to the pace of innovation in LLM engineering. Recommended resources include:

Research papers from arXiv (categories: cs.CL, cs.LG)

Blogs from AI research labs like OpenAI, Meta AI, Cohere, and Anthropic

Courses such as DeepLearning.AI's NLP Specialization or Hugging Face's LLM Practical Course

Community platforms like GitHub, Reddit's /r/MachineLearning, and Discord channels for developers

Reading model cards and training logs of public models also provides insight into real-world training strategies, limitations, and best practices.

● **Career Pathways**

LLM engineering roles vary across organizations. In startups, engineers are often full-stack contributors building both the model pipelines and user interfaces. In larger companies, roles can be more specialized—such as model compression engineer, inference optimization engineer, or NLP systems architect.

Job titles might include Machine Learning Engineer, Applied Scientist, AI Systems

Developer, or LLM Platform Engineer. Roles span across sectors: tech companies, finance, healthcare, legal tech, and even government agencies. As more applications adopt private and on-device models, opportunities in edge computing, privacy-preserving machine learning, and AI ethics will continue to grow.

CONCLUSION

Over the course of this guide, we've dissected the core components, systems, practices, and frameworks essential to mastering large language model (LLM) engineering. The focus has remained grounded in practical, hands-on approaches to building and optimizing local LLM-powered applications that run effectively on edge devices or within user-owned infrastructure.

● **Recap of Key Insights**

1. Understanding LLM Fundamentals: Developers must understand how LLMs work under the hood. These models are built on deep learning, particularly transformer architectures. Their strength lies in their ability to encode semantic relationships through attention mechanisms,

which allow them to process and generate human-like language. This core functionality is the basis of everything built on top of an LLM.

2. The Case for Local LLMs: Running models locally has distinct advantages. It minimizes latency, offers offline functionality, reduces cloud dependency, and strengthens data privacy. This is particularly critical in industries where compliance with data protection regulations is non-negotiable. With the advent of quantization, pruning, and distillation techniques, large models can now be reduced in size and optimized for local execution.

3. Toolchains and Frameworks: A robust development environment is foundational. Tools like PyTorch, Hugging Face Transformers, ONNX Runtime, and GGUF-

compatible frameworks empower developers to efficiently build, fine-tune, and deploy LLMs. Understanding containerization, GPU acceleration, and resource management is vital for ensuring consistent performance across different environments.

4. Model Customization and Fine-Tuning: Adaptability is key. General-purpose models often require domain-specific fine-tuning to align outputs with application-specific requirements. Techniques like supervised fine-tuning, reinforcement learning from human feedback (RLHF), and low-rank adaptation (LoRA) have been introduced to optimize models while reducing the computational footprint.

5. Performance Optimization: Whether deploying on mobile, desktop, or edge

servers, performance is critical. Developers must benchmark models under realistic conditions and apply optimization strategies such as mixed-precision inference, tensor decomposition, memory mapping, and thread-level parallelism. Balancing model accuracy with latency and throughput constraints is a core challenge.

6. Smart App Integration: Successful implementation goes beyond raw inference. Designing seamless human-computer interaction requires UX integration, state management, and feedback loops that enable context-aware responses. These features define the perceived intelligence of an LLM-powered app.

7. Data Security and Compliance: Local LLMs bring significant advantages in data governance. Applications processing

healthcare records, financial transactions, or personal identifiers benefit from keeping all processing on-device. Techniques such as encrypted storage, secure enclaves, and federated fine-tuning contribute to a robust security posture.

8. Scaling and Cross-Platform Strategies: Scaling local models isn't about increasing size but extending applicability. Developers can design modular architectures that reuse model capabilities across platforms. Using WebAssembly (WASM), TensorFlow Lite, and platform-specific APIs allows consistent performance on mobile, browser, and embedded systems.

9. Robust Debugging and Testing: Building reliable LLM apps requires more than clean code. Robustness must be validated against edge cases, malformed inputs, and

adversarial prompts. Logging, assertions, model introspection, and continuous evaluation pipelines are essential to catch regressions and maintain model quality.

10. Staying Ahead: The field is advancing rapidly. Lightweight model architectures like Phi-3, Mixtral, and TinyLLaMA are pushing the boundaries of what can run locally. Keeping track of open-source innovations, staying involved in developer communities, and experimenting with the latest training and quantization methods is essential for maintaining relevance in this space.

- **Final Thoughts on LLM Engineering and its Impact on App Development**

The integration of LLMs into software development is redefining the boundaries of what applications can do. Language models introduce an abstraction layer capable of interpreting intent, generating dynamic content, understanding user context, and performing reasoning tasks that previously required hand-coded logic or human input. This shift transforms apps from static tools into adaptive systems capable of real-time learning and interaction.

For developers, this means adopting a new mental model. Application logic now includes probabilistic components. Outputs are no longer deterministic functions of inputs but generated sequences influenced by token probability distributions. Debugging, performance evaluation, and user feedback must be reinterpreted in this context. The demand for local LLMs is driven by infrastructure decentralization, privacy concerns, and increasing edge computing capabilities. Smartphones, laptops, and even microcontrollers are now equipped to run trimmed-down models. This opens opportunities for innovation in personal assistants, offline analytics, autonomous agents, and low-latency decision-making systems.

The impact extends across sectors:

- Healthcare: Secure on-device diagnostics, clinical note generation, and patient communication.

- Finance: Local models for fraud detection, personalized financial advice, and secure audit trails.

- Education: Personalized tutoring systems that work offline and respect student data privacy.

- Manufacturing: Predictive maintenance and quality control systems embedded in factory equipment.

- Legal: Contract analysis and summarization tools deployed within firms, maintaining confidentiality.

These applications do not rely solely on novelty. Their success hinges on thoughtful design, rigorous optimization, and strategic deployment. As compute democratizes and open-source models become more powerful, the playing field for innovation expands.

● Encouragement to Start Developing with LLMs

There is no shortage of entry points. Whether you're building a chatbot, automating internal workflows, or experimenting with creative applications, the ecosystem is rich with resources. Pre-trained models are widely available, tooling has matured, and deployment pathways are well-documented.

Begin by identifying a problem domain. Choose a model architecture that aligns with the problem's complexity. Prototype quickly using pre-trained models and refine through iterative evaluation. Consider how your application handles inputs, structures outputs, and adapts to user interactions.

Experimentation is essential. Many assumptions about what LLMs can and cannot do are being rewritten. Keep your scope manageable but ambitious. Integrate evaluation loops to measure impact over time. Remember that quality is determined not by novelty, but by how well the system meets user needs.

Use open-source projects to accelerate development. Communities such as Hugging Face, LM Studio, Ollama, and LangChain offer repositories, tools, and active support channels. Contributing back helps improve the ecosystem and builds your credibility in the field.

Consider running tests on real devices, in real-world conditions. A model that performs well on a developer workstation may behave differently on a battery-constrained mobile device. Resource profiling, power analysis, and failover mechanisms are just as important as the model's intelligence.

Model weight sharing, collaboration with domain experts, and feedback from real users often accelerate progress more than brute-force experimentation. Treat LLM engineering as a multidisciplinary practice that combines software architecture, machine learning, UX design, and system optimization.

Call to Action

The frontier is open. Local LLM engineering is not confined to research labs or large tech companies. It is accessible to independent developers, startup teams, and internal innovation units. The tools are mature enough, the models are powerful enough, and the infrastructure is flexible enough.

Build something functional, even if simple. A working prototype teaches more than a dozen papers. Each iteration uncovers new performance considerations, user interaction challenges, and model limitations. These insights are invaluable.

Document your progress. Share your findings. Publish experiments, open-source your tools, and write technical articles. Your work will contribute to a growing body of knowledge that helps others navigate the same path.

Local LLMs represent a shift toward user-controlled intelligence. They decentralize AI, bring computation closer to the user, and prioritize privacy and performance. Engineering them well requires diligence, creativity, and respect for constraints. But the payoff is substantial: smarter applications, empowered users, and a more open technological future.

Start building.